# Beaver and Squirrel

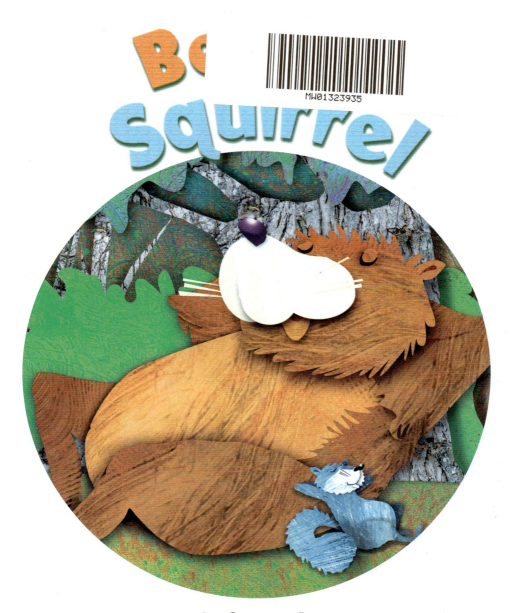

by Gustavo Juana
Illustrated by Susan Swan

Glenview, Illinois • Boston, Massachusetts • Chandler, Arizona
Upper Saddle River, New Jersey

"Hello Squirrel!" says Bear.
Bear and Squirrel are friends.
They live in the forest.

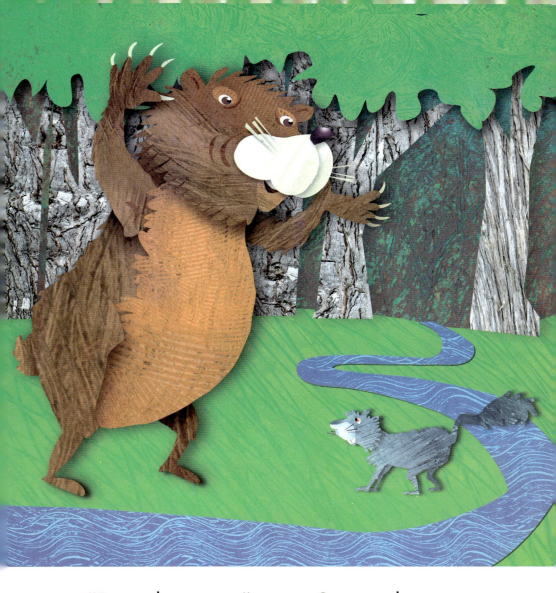

"I am hungry," says Squirrel.
"We can look for food," says Bear.

Squirrel sees some bugs.
They are under leaves.
Squirrel eats the bugs.

Bear sees some berries.
They are next to the stream.
Bear eats the berries.

Squirrel eats some nuts.
They are in the tree.
"I am full," says Squirrel.

Bear eats some fish.
They are in the stream.
"I am full too," says Bear.

Bear and Squirrel are tired.
They sleep under a tree.